Falling down can help us free ourselves

from the unnecessary.

First published in Belgium and Holland by Clavis Uitgeverij, Hasselt – Amsterdam, 2008
Copyright © 2008, Clavis Uitgeverij

English translation from the Dutch by Clavis Publishing Inc. New York
Copyright © 2009 for the English language edition: Clavis Publishing Inc. New York

Visit us on the web at www.clavis-publishing.com

For Those Who Want to Fly written and illustrated by Pirkko Vainio
Original title: *Voor wie wil vliegen*
Translated from the Dutch by Clavis Publishing

ISBN 978-1-60537-032-3

This book was printed in July 2019 at Grafiche AZ srl,
Viale del Lavoro 8, I-37036 San Martino Buon Albergo - Verona - Italy

First Edition
10 9 8

Clavis Publishing supports the First Amendment and celebrates the right to read

PIRKKO VAINIO

For Those Who Want to Fly

NEW YORK

Each of us have our own way

of facing the world.

Sometimes our past prevents us

from seeing where we are going.

The lengths of our shadows depend on

the position of the sun.

Jumping high is not yet flying.

Our own growth cannot be

compared to another's appearance.

All reflections are inaccurate,

but they make us dream.

Happy moments make our feet

feel like flowers.

Having wings does not necessarily mean

we can fly … yet!

Failure wakes up our will.

Being afraid of getting hurt

puts us in uncomfortable positions.

Bravery often means being strong

enough to accept our own weaknesses.

Letting go consciously

teaches us the precious art of landing.

Fighting for our freedom

develops all our capabilities.

When they offer you help,

assert yourself - you are not prey.

Creative experiments are seldom

applauded by the public.

Observing others is useful,

but never lose your individuality.

You're entitled to rest,

so don't worry about what others do.

Patience is certainly not the quickest

way to reach the top, but it will increase

your self-control.

Borrowing someone else's equipment

won't improve your own abilities.

Instead of thinking about what you're missing, enjoy imagining what you'll be able to do one day.

You don't have to reach the stars,

for dreaming brings you to the sky.